Church Planting Primer

Church Planting Primer

Why New Churches Are Needed
and How They Are Started

Clint Clifton

Copyright © 2017 Clint Clifton
All rights reserved.

ISBN-13: 9780692807798
ISBN-10: 0692807799

TABLE OF CONTENTS

Preface vii
Introduction ix

Chapter One   A Biblical Rationale for
                          Church Planting. 1
Chapter Two   The Need for New Churches . .16
Chapter Three How New Churches Begin 34
Chapter Four   How Ordinary Christians
                          Can Begin New Churches. . . 47

Conclusion 71
Endnotes 75

PREFACE

Hi there, my name is Clint Clifton. I began following Jesus when I was 15 years old. From my earliest discipleship meetings with my pastor, he challenged me to use the one short life God gave me to spread the Gospel. As I began to give my life to that work, I quickly realized that church planting was the best way to spread the Gospel. Over the past 20 years, I've watched God use the zeal and faith of ordinary Christians to raise up new churches in hard places. I have seen those churches produce a steady stream of new disciples in their communities. I'm convinced there is no more effective use of a Christian's life than to work to establish and renew local churches wherever we find them lacking.

What I've found is that many, if not most modern American Christians know very little about church planting. This book is designed to be a brief introduction to the "why's" and "how's" of church planting.

I'd like to thank you for your willingness to explore the content of this book. *Church Planting Primer* is also made a class based on this material. All of the videos, manuscripts, and student outlines are available and completely free online in order to encourage churches to use and share the content with their own congregations. To access these materials, visit us at newcityplanting.org/primer._

INTRODUCTION

As a brand new Christian I had the good fortune of becoming a member of a small church a mile or two from my childhood home. The church's pastor, Dannie, noticed me and took a special interest in helping me grow. A woman named Nancy saw that I was struggling academically and took it upon herself to help me become successful in school. Hovey gave me a job at the dry cleaners he owned, and taught me the value of hard work. Vivian gave me a very personal gift and told me that she believed God would use me to be a great pastor someday. Bobby paid my tuition with proceeds from his towing business. Karen and Candy alternated giving me a ride to school each day. Carl sold me my first car (well under market value), and Raymond gave me my second car when the first one broke down. Jody taught me to pray; Greg taught me to sing; Terry gave me his daughter. Countless meals, dozens of life altering conversations, mountains of encouragement, and moments of rebuke—all of this because of my membership to a local church.

Looking back on the last twenty years of my Christian life, I can say with sincerity that no institution has had as much lasting and dramatic impact on my life as the church I was a part of when I became a Christian. Peniel Baptist Church in Palatka, Florida discipled me, loved me, and rebuked me. They hammered me into the rough form of a man I am now.

Communities all over the world need churches. Not stale, lifeless churches, but vibrant, gospel-loving, Jesus-preaching churches; churches possessing a greater concern for the growth of the Kingdom of God than for the growth of their own congregation; churches led by faithful and Godly men. New City Network exists to aid men and women in the Metro DC area to become just that.

Church plants need Godly leaders; church plants also need Godly members. This conviction is what has given birth to Church Planting Primer. My vision for the *Primer* is to help any

Christian on their way to becoming either. There is one thing I know about any person that is reading this: they long to be a part of something that matters. Friends, church planting matters. As you read this book, I pray you feel God stirring in you, either to become a church planter, or to leverage your life in support of church plants; in doing so, you will be fulfilling the final marching order of Jesus Christ himself ([Matthew 28:18-20](#)).

CHAPTER ONE

A BIBLICAL RATIONALE FOR CHURCH PLANTING

Have you ever considered the incredible odds against Christianity? The self-proclaimed Son of God and his rag-tag band of merry misfits first preached the Gospel on the other side of the world and, somehow, it made its way all over the globe. From Israel it spread north, south, east and west. It crossed oceans and climbed mountains; it traveled on the backs of horses, donkeys, and camels. The Gospel has traversed every imaginable terrain to make its way to you and me. This was all made possible because of small churches.

Within just a few short generations, Christianity grew from an obscure regional uprising into a worldwide movement. It happened through the multiplication of churches. These churches didn't look like much at first, and the men and women who led them didn't have much training or ministry experience. These tenacious men and women stood boldly in the face of famine, persecution, and physical peril.

Picture a scrappy weed bursting through a crack in the median of a city street. It stubbornly pushes its way toward the sun. Think of the odds against which this weed sprouted. Its unwelcoming environment includes the constant buzz from traffic, smog, oil, litter, heat – not to mention the fact that there is virtually no nourishment – yet, there it is, stubbornly growing and stretching for the light above. City road weeds are nature's equivalent of the church. Somehow the church thrives in distress and danger; somehow it grows without abundant resources. Like weeds, with great effort and striving, churches make it! Doesn't that make you want to cheer on these Gospel sprouts?

As we begin to consider the task of building God's church, let us remember that it is under the sovereign rule and protection of God. It will break through the hardest of concrete in due time.

Mark Dever, pastor of Capitol Hill Baptist Church in Washington D.C. describes church planting this way:

> *"Church Planting is the normal business of the local church… It is where Christians are taught to obey everything Jesus commanded."*[1] – Mark Dever

The majority of Christians like the idea of church planting – conceptually, at least. Even so, the vast majority of Christians and churches will never start a church or even give serious consideration to doing so. Oftentimes, church leaders are so busy growing the ministries entrusted to them that they don't have time to think about starting new churches. One reason that many Christians do not more readily consider planting churches is that they are unaware of the strong biblical mandate to plant churches. They simply do not know that the Bible commands Christians to start new churches. However, just because the average Christian doesn't know where to find scriptural support for church planting, doesn't mean that there is none. So let's start our study together by looking at the biblical rationale for church planting.

Church Planting is Important Because the Church is Important

Farming matters because food matters. Hospitals matter because people matter. Church planting matters because the church matters. Not everyone sees it that way, though. Even some professing Christians don't think the church is really very important at all.[2]

Many in our society consider churches to be irrelevant, corrupt, antiquated, and contentious (which of course is partially true). Civic and governmental authorities often consider churches as special interest groups that hinder municipal progress and profit.

Does this make the church irrelevant? No. Nothing could be further from the truth! Jesus' church is the most important institution in the history of the world because Jesus is the most important figure in human history. When all of the world's books are closed and time yields to eternity, the church will be celebrated as the most significant institution in human history. Authors Kevin DeYoung and Ted Kluck write:

> *We love the church because Christ loved the church. She is his bride – a harlot at times, but his bride nonetheless, being washed clean*

> *by the word of God (Eph. 5:25-26). If you are into Jesus, don't rail on his bride. Jesus died for the church, so don't be bothered by a little dying to self for the church's sake. If you keep in mind that everyone there is a sinner (including yourself) and that Jesus Christ is the point and not you, your dreams, or your kids, your church experience might not be as lame as you fear.[3]*

CHURCH PLANTING IN THE BIBLE

Though you will not find the term "church planting" explicitly written in the Bible, that doesn't mean that church planting is not a biblical idea. If you're looking for it, you'll see church planting all over the New Testament. For example:

JESUS

Jesus, the hero of the Bible, established the universal Church, and declared that the gates of hell would not prevail against it (Matthew 16:18). He also led a small congregation of disciples, teaching them the Word of God, sharing communion with them, and commissioning them to plant more churches.

Paul

His commissioning by the church at Antioch in Acts 13 marks the beginning of an incredible church-planting streak by the great apostle. Over the course of 13 years, Paul embarked on three missionary journeys, during which he traveled more than 7,000 miles and planted at least 14 new churches.

The Apostles

The Apostles themselves were church planters, and the book of Acts is an account of their church-planting ministry. They planted churches with little support from other churches and in the face of great political and religious opposition. Ultimately, their commitment to obey the Great Commission by planting churches cost them their lives.

The Great Commission

Spoken by Jesus in Matthew 28:19-20, the Great Commission is essentially a call to plant new churches. We can say this because baptizing, teaching, and making disciples are exactly what churches are called to do throughout the rest of the New Testament! Additionally, the dozen men who originally heard Jesus say the words "baptize, teach, and make disciples" responded by spending the rest of their lives organizing new churches.

Church Planting in Acts

In the book of Acts alone we find dozens of references to church planting. In fact, the book itself is the story of the *founding* of the New Testament church. Dave Bruskas highlights a few of the church planting high-points in the book of Acts:

- *Jesus sent his Apostles to plant the first church in Jerusalem. ([Acts 1:8](#), [2:1-47](#))*
- *Philip preached the Gospel in Samaria, compelling the members of the Jerusalem church to share the Gospel elsewhere. ([Acts 8:4-24](#)).*
- *Saul (Paul), the greatest missionary the world has ever known, was converted from a church persecutor to a church planter. ([Acts 9](#))*
- *Barnabas was sent by the Jerusalem church plant and led the church at Antioch. ([Acts 11:19-26](#))*

- *Paul and Barnabas were called directly by the Holy Spirit on mission to launch new churches, and the church prayed, fasted, and affirmed their calling.* (Acts 13:1-4)
- *Paul's missionary ministry of planting churches forms the rest of the story of Acts as he preached the Gospel in every city, planted new churches, and remained until elders were in place to shepherd the flock* (Acts 14:23, Titus 1:5).[4]

Additionally, many of the New Testament letters were written to encourage, rebuke, or instruct church planters and their congregations. The majority of the prominent New Testament characters are church planters or members of church planting teams.

A Comprehensive Case

Like many doctrines in the Bible, the most compelling case for church planting is found in a synthesis of Scripture, not in any one verse. The phrase "church planting" is not mentioned in the Bible, but then again neither is the word "Trinity." Does that mean that the Trinity isn't scriptural? Of course not! The synthesis of many texts leads us to a clearer understanding of the Trinity. The same is true for church planting.

Virtually every evangelistic church in North America would agree that the Great Commission applies to all churches, and that all churches and all Christians should endeavor to fulfill the Great Commission. Yet, far fewer are able to accept that every church and every Christian should be involved in church planting. This perspective contradicts Scripture. *It is important to realize that the Great Commission is fulfilled by church planting, and the Great Commission cannot be properly fulfilled without planting churches.*

You may think that's a bold statement, but here are two reasons to absolutely convince you that the Great Commission is a call to start new churches. First, the substance of the Great Commission is "Go, Baptize, Teach, and Make Disciples." Those are the substantive activities of the local church. No other organization or entity on the planet has as its job description to baptize new believers, teach all the things Jesus commanded, and make disciples for Jesus. Second, the apostles who heard Jesus say, "Go, therefore, and make disciples of all nations baptizing them in the name of the Father,

Son and Holy Spirit," responded to Jesus' commission by planting churches!

If the apostles heard the Great Commission and responded by planting churches, then what should we do when we hear the Great Commission? Should we respond in some other way? Who has misunderstood the Great Commission, the apostles or modern believers?

When we plant a new church, it's like setting up a disciple-making factory in a community that will soon be churning out new disciples of Jesus all the time. Planting a new church is like installing a new door into the kingdom of heaven, giving a new access point to God for our lost friends and family members.

In 1845 the great preacher Charles Spurgeon spoke to his congregation about the issue of church planting in this way:

> *"We encourage our members to leave us to found other Churches; nay, we seek to persuade them to do it. We ask them to scatter throughout the land to become the goodly seed, which God shall bless. I believe that so long as we do this we shall prosper."[5]*

Church Planter Testimony:
Kenji Adachi

I'm Kenji Adachi, a church planter with All Peoples Community Church in Fairfax, Va. I am married (with one wife!), and three kids. God has called me to plant a church to reach the people here in the Fairfax area. I didn't grow up in a Christian home. I didn't grow up "churched." I didn't trust Jesus until I was 16 years old. So, my heart is for lost peoples.

I grew up in Greensboro, NC. All of my friends in my neighborhood were white, and they bussed us, to integrate us, to a black school inside the city. So here I am, I have a context where my friends are either white or black, and I'm able to flow with these relationships. They looked at me, and…they didn't know what to think of me because, in North Carolina, there are more churches than there are Asians! Then, God brought me here, to Fairfax, VA where there are so many Asians in this area, and that context has enabled me to go from white, to black, to now Asian—back to my roots—and to be able to identify with these people and reach these people contextually with the Gospel.

I was serving at a church for 12 years in this area, but God placed a big burden on my heart to plant churches—not just to plant churches for the sake of starting something new—but really because it is the single most effective way to reach lost people. And not just lost people, but the types of people that are here. People that are new, people that are unchurched, the younger, millennial generation, people that are of different ethnic groups; and when I think about my ministry over the previous 12 years in my previous church, all the things that God stirred in my heart, what I longed for and lived and ministered to, it was these same types of people: younger people, lost people, internationals, and new people. That's why I'm planting a church, to reach these types of people.

When we look at the Bible, Paul was the ultimate church planter. He would go to strategic cities and he would plant churches. He was fulfilling Jesus' command for the Great Commission of going and making disciples. If we ask, "How do we do that?" When we look at the biblical model we see what was effective was planting multiplying churches and reaching people in that specific context, whether that was Ephesus, or Rome, or Crete, or wherever it may be, by raising up indigenous leaders who are a part of that city, to reach that city.

One of the greatest challenges of church planting is leaving what is comfortable and secure. I have a family with three kids. My wife and I have been married coming up now on 20 years. She is sick with Lyme Disease, and for God to call me to leave all of that stability and to do this, it's not something that I would encourage for anyone—but, if you're called, we must obey.

What does that look like for me? My wife said this, "It feels like jumping off a cliff." But for someone like me, I love jumping off of cliffs, if Jesus is calling me to do that. But it's hard for my family. It's hard for my kids. You know, they are having to jump with me. I'm not pulling them; we're doing this together. And, they are seeing God's faithfulness through this. God has financially provided in miraculous ways. We are seeing God increase in who he is, how holy and how awesome that he is, and if I were to do it again I wouldn't do it differently just for this experience. And not necessarily just for planting the church, but for allowing my family to see God's faithfulness and his grace.

Our hope is to plant a church that is holistic; that really makes a difference in the community, to bless all peoples. It's not necessarily a church for ourselves so we can see, "Oh, look at the numbers, or the attendance, or the giving, or all that." It's not to say "Look what we're doing." We want people in the community to say the very same thing when they go to the grocery store; if this grocery store were ever to leave they would say "Why are you leaving? We need this grocery store." We want that kind of Gospel impact, that the Lord would use us to save people, of course, but also to love them, connect them together, equip them, and to send them out that they may be a blessing in the community as well. I think it's one of the most exciting things you could ever go on, to be able to start something from scratch, to be there from the very beginning, and to see people come to faith in Christ, mature in faith together as a church family, to start something new and to make an impact in a community.

We need people that are mature in their faith. We need generous people. We need gifted people. We need people to come on board to help us do something like this, to reach their community; don't they want to reach their neighbors, their coworkers? That's my desire! That's why I'm planting this church, because I want to see the Gospel go forward and touch people's lives. We definitely need all kinds of support and prayer, obviously. We need financial support. We need people from the outside that may have all sorts of gifting's that can make videos, or help with a website, or can help with children's ministry, or maybe be a short-term missionary in the community. Maybe they give 6 months of their time, or a year to serve our children's ministry, or play on the worship team, or whatever it may be that helps free up the core people of the church plant.

Church planting isn't just for pioneers, people that are crazy and step out in faith. It's really for everybody. It's for the regular Joe that is established and part of the life of a regular church. They can also be a part of a church planting movement by thinking, not just about their church, but also about their city; how can we strategically reach this city? I've been blessed that God has brought faithful people, people that believe not just in the vision, but love me and support. That's what I need more than just people doing things. Church planters need people. You don't have to be a part of the All-Star Team. We're not looking for the Green Berets of church planting. We're looking for faithful people that will love well, and serve the Lord faithfully.

CHAPTER TWO

THE NEED FOR NEW CHURCHES

> *A net gain of 3,205 churches is needed each year for the American church to keep up with population growth; this is far [greater] than the actual yearly gain.*[6]
> – DAVID T. OLSON

It is my observation that people rarely consider how churches begin—but, almost never consider how they end. Churches, just like people, have life cycles. They are born and they die. They close their doors, they sell their buildings, they liquidate their assets, and they stop gathering. If you don't believe me, get on a plane to Jerusalem and look for the church first pastored by James. Then skip over to Turkey and see if you can still find the church meeting at Antioch. Those churches closed, disbanded, and scattered.

American churches are closing too, and not just one or two at a time – they are closing by the thousands. This Sunday morning when you go to church, about 135 fewer American churches will be gathering than did the same time last week. That is 600 churches disbanding every month and 7,000 churches melting under the heat of an increasingly secular society each year.[7]

You see, church planting is important not just because the church is important but:

Church Planting is Important Because the Church is Dwindling

Imagine if the human race were in the same predicament. It would be disturbing and unsettling, and my guess is that people would become aggressively proactive about repopulating the world. The church in America is in this exact predicament. We are an endangered species; if nothing changes, the America of the future will look very similar to the Western Europe of today.

Today the streets of major cities throughout Western Europe are peppered with church buildings that lasted longer than the congregations that erected them. Hundreds of church buildings are now being used as restaurants, nightclubs, concert venues, cafés, modern condominiums, museums, and mosques. They stand as proof that western culture is spitting Christianity out of its mouth. The Huffington Post reports,

> "Between the years 2010 and 2012, more than half of all churches in America added not one new member. Each year, nearly 3 million more previous church-goers enter the ranks of the "religiously unaffiliated."[8]

The change is not really that shocking if you think about it. Churches are made up of sinners, and sin kills everything it touches. As long as sinners are going to church, churches will be dying. As long as churches are dying, new churches are necessary. Every year in America about 4,000 evangelical churches begin.[9] Of those started, 35% close before their 5th anniversary,[10] leaving about 2,600 new churches planted annually. While churches are dying at a significantly higher rate, each year in the U.S. approximately 7,000 churches close their doors forever. All things considered, the number of churches in the U.S.

is decreasing by about 4,400 churches per year,[11] while our population is growing by about three million people per year.

Church Planting is important because most existing Churches Have plateaued or are declining

Researcher Aubrey Malphurs recalls this quote from Win Arn,

> *"Today, of the approximately 350,000 churches in America, four out of five are either plateaued or declining. Many churches begin a plateau or slow decline about their fifteenth to eighteenth year. 80-85% are on the down-side of this cycle."*[12]

You may ask, "Why not just renew dying churches?" We should help dying churches, but church renewal is not enough. We must also plant churches to reach people with the Gospel. We have to increase the "birth rate" (by planting new churches) and decrease the "death rate" (by helping old churches). We should do everything we can to help renew churches in our city that have fallen on hard times, and we should do everything we can do to plant new churches in our communities. Furthermore, revitalizing existing churches does nothing for areas without a church presence already.

What Is happening to the church?
The church is getting bigger

Individual churches are getting larger and larger. Today, the average American church has 75 members, a number that has been steadily increasing over the past few decades. Some churches are getting very large. In North America over the past 50 years, we have seen an explosion of megachurches with more than 2,000 people in attendance each weekend.

The number of megachurches in America has nearly doubled every decade over the last 50 years. In fact, researcher Ed Stetzer claims that there are as many megachurches in the Nashville area today as there were in the entire country in 1960.[13] 50% of all churches in America average less than 100 in worship attendance. 40% of all churches in America average between 100 and 350 in attendance. 10% of all churches in America average more than 350 in attendance.[14]

THE CHURCH IS GETTING SMALLER

An interesting thing happens when you start questioning folks about their church attendance. It is what researchers call the "halo effect." It is what the rest of the world calls lying. For instance, Gallup polls report that about 40% of the population claims regular church attendance, while in truth, only about 17% of Americans attend church regularly.[15] Each year the population of the United States grows, but the percentage of Americans attending church decreases. Kelly Shattuck fleshes out this reality by addressing a misperception of Kirk Hadaway and Penny Long Marler, known for their scholarly church research:

> *"We knew that over the past 30 to 40 years, denominations had increasingly reported a decline in their numbers," Marler says. "Even a still-growing denomination like the Southern Baptist Convention had reported slowed growth. Most of the mainline denominations were all reporting a net loss over the past 30 years. And at the same time, the Gallup polls had remained stable. It didn't make sense."[16]*

The statistics did not make sense because they were wrong.

The Church is Getting More Professional

The more professional the church becomes, the more unlikely it is that everyday Christians will see themselves as fit for legitimate gospel services. Though there is nothing wrong with formal training or professional vocational ministry, the church must embrace the fact that God's criteria for service in his kingdom have to do with character, not credentials.

It is important for us to remember that Jesus recruited disciples off the beach, not out of the synagogue. Formal theological training is not a prerequisite for pastoral ministry. While it may be helpful, it is not necessary. The Christian who meets the character standards for an elder explained in 1 Timothy and Titus are every bit as qualified (perhaps more qualified) for ministry than those with seminary degrees. Paul reminds Timothy that God allowed him to serve in ministry because of his faithfulness, not because of his credentials (1 Timothy 1:12).

The American church saw the greatest growth during the nation's westward expansion, both in terms of conversions and church planting.[17] These were the days of circuit-riding preachers. These missionary pastors had a high commitment to spreading the Gospel on the frontier, and required little in exchange for their work. Take the life of one circuit-riding preacher as an example:

> *Jacob Young was just 26 years old when in 1802 he took on the responsibility of forming a new Methodist circuit along the Green River in Kentucky. He had little prior training and little prospect of outside assistance. He developed his own strategy to evangelize the region: "I concluded to travel five miles... then stop, search the neighborhood and find some kind person who would let me preach in his log cabin and so on till I had performed the entire round." On a number of occasions, he found groups already gathered, waiting for a preacher to arrive. Wherever he could, he established class meetings run by local leaders to carry on the work in his absence. In one location he discovered a society run by Jacob,*

> *an illiterate African-American slave. Jacob's preaching and leadership impressed Young. By the end of his first year as a circuit-rider Young had gathered 301 new members and for his efforts received just $30 – a cost of 10 cents per new member. Circuit-riders like Jacob Young began with little formal education. But they soon became students as they followed the example of Wesley and Asbury who used their time on horseback for reading.[18]*

It would be rare to find a pastor in North America today with the commitment and evangelistic fervor that Jacob Young and his circuit-riding peers had. In just a few generations, this saddle-slinging, rough-and-tumble, cowboy-pastor-that-works-for-free had been replaced by the modern, professional pastor.

> *Professionalism has nothing to do with the essence and the heart of the Christian ministry. The more professional we long to be, the more spiritual death we will leave in our wake. For there is no professional childlikeness, there is no professional tenderheartedness; there is no professional panting after God. – John Piper[19]*

THE CHURCH IS GETTING MORE INCLUSIVE

Though many churches have remained faithful to the gospel message, as a whole, more churches than ever are accepting doctrines and teachings of other religions as valid and acceptable. Doctrines and practices that would have been widely rejected by Christians and churches a few decades ago are widely accepted today. As doctrinal clarity fades from the Christian church, and the distinction between the world and the church is harder to see, the church's usefulness is called into question.

THE CHURCH IS GETTING LESS EFFECTIVE

Many denominations and groups are reporting a steady decline in baptisms. The Southern Baptist Convention, for instance, has seen a steady decline in the numbers of baptisms since 1999, down by nearly 100,000 baptisms in the past 15 years.[20] Other denominations are reporting similar statistics. So what do we do about it? **We plant churches!**

> *"The vigorous, continual planting of new congregations is the single most crucial strategy for 1) the numerical growth of the Body of Christ in any city, and 2) the continual corporate renewal and revival of the existing churches in a city.*

> *Nothing else–not crusades, outreach programs, para-church ministries, growing mega-churches, congregational consulting, nor church renewal processes–will have the consistent impact of dynamic, extensive church planting. – Tim Keller [21]*

COMMON OBJECTIONS TO CHURCH PLANTING

I often ask pastors I meet if they have ever led their church to plant a new church. Although most have not, they have a positive view of church planting. They commonly express to me their desire to lead their congregation to plant new churches. When I ask why they haven't, I generally get the same few responses:

"WE JUST DON'T HAVE THE PEOPLE TO SEND."

Usually what is really meant is, "We have a bunch of ministries now that are understaffed. We will have to wait until all the ministries are staffed. When that impossible task is accomplished, we will consider starting a new church." This is teaching people that fulfilling Jesus' mission is equal to staffing the ministries of our church. It is not necessary or even possible for your church to be perfect before you obey the Bible's command to spread the Gospel.

"WE DON'T HAVE THE MONEY."
Church planting is only expensive because we think that, in order to have a legitimate church, it has to begin with a five-piece worship band, a modern facility, a sophisticated sound system, and theater lighting to set the mood. How much does it cost to share the Gospel with your neighbor? How much does it cost to meet in your living room? Church planting is about making, baptizing, and teaching disciples – all of which are free! Using money on ministry is not bad. In many ways, money can enhance our ministry, but money is not required to raise up new leaders for gospel ministry. The vast majority of pastors in the world are volunteer or bi-vocational pastors who somehow find a way to conduct meaningful ministry with little to no money.

"OUR PEOPLE AREN'T READY FOR THAT YET."
This one may be legitimate for a time. Some congregations are genuinely not ready, but priority

number one should be to get them ready. Mission is at the center of God's design for the church, so we have to make Ephesians 4:12 the job description of every pastor: "Equip the saints for the work of the ministry."

"I DON'T FEEL GOD LEADING US IN THAT DIRECTION."

If you do not feel God leading you to obey the Great Commission, it is possible that you are relying more on your own desires for ministry than the desires God expresses in His Word. A strong commitment to the Great Commission will be required in order to lead any church to give away resources that could be used for the growth of their own congregation. Many people say that they are going to wait until they reach 300 or 500 or 1,000 attendees before they start a new church, believing it will be easier then. Church planting does not get easier as time goes on and churches get larger. In fact, it gets harder. Once a church begins thinking primarily about itself – its growth, its comfort, and its facilities – turning its attention back to reproduction is nearly impossible. There is no better way for a congregation to stay focused on the mission of spreading the Gospel than to lead them to plant other churches early and often.

Church Planter Testimony: Brian Collison

I'm Brian Collison, and I'm planting a church right outside of Ft. Belvoir army installation in Alexandria, Va. I served on active duty in the Army for about ten years. During that time, I served as a medic, and as a criminal investigator. As a criminal investigator I spent everybody's worst day ever with them, and I really didn't want to be on the back-end always reacting to their worst day. I wanted to be able to give them counsel. I saw God leading me more into counseling, specifically Biblical counseling. I left active duty in 2010 so that I could go to seminary so that I could prepare for a career in Biblical counseling. God began to really shape me during that time. I didn't really have a preconceived notion of what my career field or what my job was really going to look like. I just wanted to be available to God. He kind of plucked me out of that and mobilized me again with the Army reserves in 2013 to come up to Ft. Belvoir and work in Washington DC for a little bit.

While I was in DC, I got plugged in with a church that had a heart, not just for church planting, but for planting churches near military installations, which really spoke to me. I made the mistake of saying, "What about the Army? What about Army church planting?" That began the journey of me getting challenged, not only by my local pastor, but by a lot of the folks that were in my circle of influence to think about "How was I going to make an impact on the military, and the folks in my sphere of influence with the gospel in a local church setting."

I really didn't feel like I had the gifts or the abilities that were needed for church planting. I had this idea of what I thought a church planter looked like, and it didn't match what I saw in the mirror. But, there were guys around me that were really starting to challenge me, and starting to draw things out of me to show me it wasn't about me, it was about the team that God would bring around me. I had no idea how all of that would come together. Just the simple fact of looking for a place to meet, who would be apart that core group that would come together to see the work done, I felt unprepared myself to lead this kind of work. I always saw myself as a team member, maybe. But, anywhere I felt a deficiency, God would plug someone in that would meet that need in the life of the church. Anywhere I felt like I would struggle, God brought someone around me that could help to not only improve my own ability, but would bring others alongside me that could show, teach, and mentor me through a process.

I am not just a lone guy leading a church plant. This is a group of folks that have come together to see

God work through them in the capacity of the local church. As I began to really feel challenged and really feel called of God to come and do this work, and as I began to pray, I really had some concerns that my wife would not feel led to come and do this work. But, as we began to talk about it, as we began to pray about it together, I realized really quickly that she was aware of gifting's in me that I didn't even know I had. She was willing to step out in faith for her own life as a part of her own discipleship. So, I have been able to grow not just as a church leader, and not just as a pastor, but as a husband and as a father as I've led a church and led my family into this process. It's been amazing to see how my kids can be a part of this. They don't feel like this is "dad's job." They feel like we are a family of missionaries that are seeing this church begin to form.

In just a few months, we have seen God grow this local church that he is putting together piece by piece. That's really been exciting for me and my family. It wasn't that long ago that I was that person that was sitting in church, in a Sunday school or a small group, that really didn't know what God was going to do with my life. I wanted to be a good church member. I wanted to be used however God saw a need. Sometimes I was stepping out and doing things that I really didn't want to do, but I knew there was a need and I knew God was calling me to do things, and I knew that there were people around me that could assist me and help me, and that was not just a way to see the church grow but also as a way to see me grow personally as a disciple of Jesus Christ.

I believe that God raises people up. He's already brought a guy that is excited about planting a church near a military community. He wants to come and spend a year or two with us, and learn what that looks like and to prepare himself and his family. So we're excited to see that happen! Just as we want our local church that we planted to get healthy and of course to grow and reach into the community that God has planted us, we also know that we can do that elsewhere, and the resources God gives us he wants us to hold on loosely, and pass those along to wherever they're needed.

We are going to do everything that we can with the resources that we have to see churches planted near and far; right outside of our community and beyond. That's really what we're most excited about, to see what God is going to do with these soldiers and sailors and family members that are going to come through our doors, and, two or three years down the road, move on and hopefully go on to plant a church somewhere else as they leave us and go and take the gospel where God leads them.

CHAPTER THREE

HOW NEW CHURCHES BEGIN

> *Church attendance is as vital to a disciple as a transfusion of rich, healthy blood to a sick man.*
> – *Dwight L. Moody*

One aim of this book is to open your mind to the possibility that God might use you to help plant a new church. It is possible that God would call you to a change in profession, but it is also entirely possible that God might use you in your current profession. As you are introduced to a bi-vocational church planting team, consider new ways God could use you to make himself known.

In this section we're going to explore how new churches begin. First, we'll examine modern and biblical church planting models. Then we'll tackle specifically how one goes about starting a new church. Let's turn our attention first to the common ways churches are being started in North America today.

7 Modern Church Planting Models
Parachute Planting:
A planter and his family move into a new location to start a church from scratch. The planter has very little connection with or existing support within the new area. The planter and his family are "pioneering" new territory. Where there is great risk, there may be great reward, but this approach is not for the faint of heart.

Sent by an existing Church:
An existing church or church planting organization provides the initial leadership and resources (funds, people, etc.) to start a new church, including the selection of the church planter. Often the church planter is selected from within the organization and has already bought into the vision, values, and beliefs of the sponsoring organization. The existing relationship allows for a close working relationship between the

"mother" and "daughter" churches. Although the new church is autonomous, the sponsoring organization often has significant influence in the new church (including decision making during the pre-launch phase). Advantages often include increased financial resources and the ability to draw core team/launch team members from the sponsoring organization.

Partnership Between Organizations:

This is a rapidly growing trend where an organization (or many organizations) committed to church planting implement a plan to plant churches. These informal alliances are referred to as collaborative or partnership networks. The participating organizations often share common beliefs and a passion for starting new churches.

House Church:

Small groups/cells (5-20 people) form and multiply via a network of people meeting in homes. In some cases, the individual cells are connected in a larger network that meets together periodically in a large group setting. This relational model focuses on personal growth, care, and teaching through one-on-one and small group discipleship. Groups are birthed through multiplication, and, often die, only to resurface months or even years later. This model requires very little funding.

MULTI-SITE CHURCH:

An existing church opens new locations. The idea is for one church to have many meeting locations. Motives range from reaching more lost people to making more room at an existing location. The multi-site movement that has taken root over the past 30 years in North America has renewed the vision of reaching entire regions or cities with a single church and has jumpstarted the missionary impulse of many churches.

CHURCH REPLANT:

An existing, struggling church decides to close in order to make room for a new church. The restart is usually in the same location under new leadership. In a church replant, the assets of an old congregation and missionary zeal of the replanter are the foundation upon which a new congregation is formed.

Church Split:
Unfortunately, this model of church planting most often results from disunity. A split typically occurs when internal disagreement leads a congregation to conclude there is less energy required to "split" or "divorce" than to resolve differences and reconcile. The underlying factors causing the split often develop over years. And, in many cases, the dysfunctional character traits of the old church carry forward into the new churches.[22]

Biblical Church Planting Models
Jerusalem Model:
A church in one location is scattered to numerous locations, and churches are planted in the places where they are scattered. Acts 11:19 clarifies, "Now those who were scattered because of the persecution that arose over Stephen traveled as far as Phoenicia and Cyprus and Antioch, speaking the word to no one except Jews." Though the believers were not scattering from Jerusalem voluntarily, they continued to be a witness for Christ, and their witness ultimately resulted in new churches.

Antioch Model:

A church sends an apostle to a town where he preaches the Gospel and organizes those who come to faith into a new church. This is the model of church planting that Paul used throughout his church planting journeys in Acts 13-20. Paul's pattern was to provide basic instruction on the Christian life and then to appoint elders to "Put in order what remains," (Titus 1:5); in other words, to organize a new church.

Ephesian Model:

A church invests time training several individuals who are then sent to plant churches. "What Paul accomplished in Ephesus was as unique as it was brilliant. He made Ephesus a training center from which the Gospel would go forth, and where young men could be trained to plant churches. Paul rented a meeting place called the Hall of Tyrannus where he preached and taught every day from 11:00am-4:00pm. This part of the training went on for two solid years.[23] The work of these Ephesian trainees led Luke to say, "All the residents of Asia heard the word of the Lord, both Jews and Greeks" (Acts 19:10).

Roman Model:
Christians from various churches coordinate their efforts to plant a church together in a new area where they form a new church. This is an effective means of church planting today. The western church is saturated with experienced and knowledgeable Christians. The redistribution of Christians to cities where the Gospel is needed in order to form new churches is the challenge of our day.

All of these models represents models churches can (and do) emulate an effort to plant churches. The World needs a lot of different types of churches, and there is no one right "model" for planting a church. This section is meant to survey the models evident in Scripture, and how some of these models do or do not cohere with modern models. After exploring modern and biblical models, it is now time to consider the types of *church planters* that might lead one of these new churches.

3 Types of Church Planters
Vocational:
Vocational planters give their vocations to God as an act of worship. They make church planting

their primary vocational pursuit, giving themselves fully to the establishment of a new church. Vocational church planters prepare for planting by saving enough money to sustain their families until the church can fully support them, or they partner with churches and other organizations that help underwrite the cost of church planting until the church reaches financial sustainability.

BI-VOCATIONAL:
Church planters may support their family through other means while working primarily for the financial, numerical, and spiritual growth of the congregation. Generally, bi-vocational planters wish to be vocational planters but are concerned about the strain a full time salary would put on a young congregation.

VOLUNTEER:
These planters continue with dedicated vocational employment in another field while simultaneously working to establish a new church. The majority of modern church planters fall into this category. Volunteer church planters are

commonly entrepreneurs, business owners, or those with flexible jobs that allow them availability throughout the workday to meet with people for evangelism, discipleship, or ministry. Ideally volunteer church planters work in the communities where they are planting a church. In such cases, their work environments give them the ability to make evangelistic contacts throughout the workday.

Church Planter Testimony:
Zack Bekele & Dawit Getachew

Zach: My name is Zechariah Bekele. I am one of the church planters among Ethiopians in the Greater DC area.

Dawit: My name is Dawit Getachew. I am one of the church planters, as well.

Zach: We are trying to reach the lost Ethiopian people in Greater DC because the evangelical presence is very low; less than 2,000 people among the 400,000 people. The need is huge.

Dawit: And Jesus told the disciples, just to go to the world, go and find the lost. The reason we are planting the church among Ethiopians around the Greater DC area is because the need is very huge. 400,000 Ethiopians live in the area, which is the second largest Ethiopian city, next to the capital of Ethiopia.

Zach: I came to U.S. in 2004. Since then, I have been involved in different capacities of church ministry. We had a lot of discussions, and we started praying. We left the city where I was, I left my job, and came here to plant a church.

Dawit: I came to the U.S. thirteen years ago, and now I'm living in Alexandria, VA. I was praying about which church I needed to go to and get involved in the church planting process. When I was praying, I met with Zack, and I heard about his church planting process. I just prayed about it. God gave me a great life, so I started getting involved in the church planting process, and I'm happy just to be part of this. Even though I'm working a full-time job in a different profession I am pleased. I think that this full-time job gives me opportunity to live in the world, but my calling is to be involved in God's Kingdom work.

Zach: In order to be a church planter, you don't need to change your profession – you don't need to stop your career. Yes, there are some people who leave their career and profession to be a full-time church planter. But as the Bible mentioned in the New Testament, we have seen people who have a different career but maintain involvement in church planting, like Aquila and Priscilla. They were tentmakers, but they were involved with Paul planting churches. They were moving to Corinth, Ephesus— wherever Paul moved, they were moving together. Even though they do a different job, they were highly involved with church planting.

Dawit: To be a church planter, you don't need to be a full-time minister. Even though you do something else vocationally, you're still involved in the church planting process. There are a lot of things to do in God's Kingdom, and I want to encourage you, even though you are not a full-timer, even though you have less time just to do God's work, go ahead and do it.

Zach: You may not think you have any role in church planting, but in one or another way, you can be involved in church planting. For example, you can pray for church planters. You may think prayer doesn't make any difference, but prayer has a huge impact in the life of the church and among church planting. You can be involved with being part of the core team of the church planter, or you can help financially. There are a lot of ways you can be involved in terms of church planting. It is not easy to win souls for Christ because people love sin. People love sin, and they are living in darkness. There is darkness in their life. So winning people for Christ is not an easy task. It needs a lot of prayer. It needs a lot of the power of the Gospel. So when the church plants start this huge task, they need help from the church. They need help from believers around the world. They need a lot of emotional encouragement. They need a lot of prayers; it's not easy. We would like to encourage you guys to encourage church planters. A church exists to plant a church, and church members exist to plant a church. And we can't do it alone, but we can do corporately.

> *Dawit: And when we plant the church, and when we're trying to do something in the church area, we're just trying to please our perfect God. It's not easy to plant a church. It's very frustrating. But let me tell you, we're called to do this. It's not about us. It's all about the One who gave us grace to do this. So, let's please God by finding the lost.*

CHAPTER FOUR

HOW ORDINARY CHRISTIANS CAN BEGIN NEW CHURCHES

Church planting does not need to be complicated or expensive, and it does not need to be done by professionals! Everyday Christians are called by God to start new churches. The requirements given by the apostle Paul for those who serve in pastoral ministry are ***character qualifications.*** The qualifications for pastoral ministry do not include experience, expertise, or education. God is looking for the holy, faithful, and humble. If church planters do not have to be professionals, and church planting does not have to be complicated or expensive, what exactly is needed to start a new church?

Only one resource is necessary for a church to begin planting another church, and it has nothing to do with buildings or budgets.

That one necessary resource is *a ready leader*. Churches are planted by missionary-pastors sent by kingdom-building churches. The only thing you absolutely must have in order to plant a new church is a scripturally qualified, missionary-pastor to send.

Where do ready leaders come from? *They are made, not born.* Talk to any successful leader about how they got where they are today, and you will hear a story of mentorship, discipleship, and investment. There are two helpful acronyms borrowed from the world of international missions that can help us recognize the right types of people to develop for a ministry in church planting.

F.A.T. People Make Great Church Planters

Paul's Ephesian church-planting model discussed in the previous chapter requires developing leaders for church planting. Therefore, finding new potential leaders for the kingdom of God is priority number one. Faithfulness, availability, and teach-ability are the essential qualities for those being developed for pastoral ministry:

Faithful

Those who are quick to obey Jesus when they know what He wants them to do are worth the investment. Some guys struggle with the same sins over and over again, and seem unwilling to take the drastic, eye-plucking, hand-chopping measures that are required to really mortify the flesh ([Matthew 5:29-30](#)). Those who are willing to take these measures inevitably grow faster and gain victory over areas of sin in their lives more quickly. There was a young man who was confessing that he was addicted to pornography. He said he would do anything to escape from its clutches. When someone asked him if he was serious enough to promise that the next time he went to a pornographic website, he would let someone toss his laptop into a creek, he stared into their face for a few seconds in deep contemplation, then promised them he would. Months later he told them that simple promise helped him gain victory over his pornography addiction. The point is God is not looking for perfect guys; He is looking for guys who are serious about obeying Jesus, even if it's costly.

Available

Consider my situation, being a pastor who lives in Northern Virginia, where everyone is always busy. Careers are demanding and traffic is atrocious. As a result, there are a plethora of excuses for not being able to meet for personal spiritual growth. When I invite someone to meet for discipleship, and they actually do it, I know that their spiritual development is a priority to them. Invest your time in those who stretch to make themselves available.

Teachable

This is perhaps the most important piece, but also the most difficult to discern at first. A person's teach-ability has to do with their willingness to implement instruction, even if they are not convinced it is credible. *The Karate Kid* offers a helpful picture. Remember when Mr. Miyagi told Daniel to paint the fence and wax the car when all Daniel wanted to do was learn Karate. Miyagi recognized some areas of Daniel's life that needed development, even though Daniel did not. The same will be true for those you disciple. Invest your time in those who heed your advice and instruction even when it does not make complete sense to them.

Consider this question for yourself: **Are you yourself faithful, available, and teachable?**

MAWL'D People Make Good Church Planters

The second acronym used when providing on-the-job training for those with ministerial aspirations is MAWL (Model, Assist, Watch, Leave). This is something you can begin doing right away with FAT people in your ministry who are eager to gain ministerial experience. The process begins with simply allowing those you are training to go with you as you accomplish the work of the ministry.

Model

If you are going to visit someone who is in the hospital, bring a FAT guy with you. If you are going to study for your sermon, invite a FAT guy to study with you. Be sure to explain everything you do, and do not hold back anything you have learned along the way. Say something like, "I try never to leave the hospital without praying for the person who is sick," or "I find that I study best in the mornings, so I set aside two mornings a week for sermon preparation." Invite a FAT guy and his family to join you and your family for devotions, or dinner, or some other opportunity that allows them see how you interact with your family. It is not rocket science. Simply invite FAT guys to see the behind-the-scenes footage of your life.

Assist
Once a particular area of ministry has been modeled, it is important to let the trainee assist. Maybe have them do some research for a sermon. Allow them to join you in teaching a section of the new members course, or to help fill up the baptistery. When it seems like they have a handle on what they are doing, start assisting *them*. Allow them to take the lead on the visitor follow up, then debrief with them after it is over.

Watch
Once it is clear that they know what they are doing, just sit back and watch. This might mean allowing a FAT guy to preach a sermon, or lead a

small group while you sit in the crowd. It might mean allowing them to put an outreach event together from start to finish. Expect that they will do it a bit differently than you, and probably not quite as well, but leaving them alone to make their own mistakes is part of the process of training. Be sure to tell them afterwards what they did well and how you think they could improve.

LEAVE

This part is critical and probably the most difficult because it requires you to get out of the way. It's a much different experience to lead something on your own without the watchful eye of a mentor in the crowd. Your presence could actually prevent those you're training from feeling fully empowered to lead. Eventually, when you feel they have a good grasp on what they are doing, leave and allow them to accomplish the task without you. As always, be sure to talk with your trainees afterward to see how things went. Give them room to grow, make mistakes, and experience firsthand some of the joys and difficulties of pastoral ministry.

Is God Calling Me to Start a New Church?

I believe there are three aspects to receiving a "calling" from God to serve in pastoral ministry. Many talk about calling as some sort of mystical, subjective experience. I believe the calling to pastoral ministry is a bit more objective than that, and includes three elements.

Aspiration

In 1 Timothy 3:1, the Apostle Paul prefaces his list of qualifications for an elder with this statement: *"If anyone aspires to the office of overseer, he desires a noble task."* The Greek word translated as "aspire" means "to stretch one's self out in order to touch or to grasp for something."[24] The word "desire" means to "long for" or "lust after."[25] Paul is saying that to be fit for the job of elder, one must stretch for it and lust after it. God is a master at producing desire where there once was apathy. The same God who wired men to desire women, and sharks to long for blood, will grant a person a voracious appetite for the spread of the Gospel. The psalmist felt this passion when he said, *"I would rather be a doorkeeper in the house of my God than dwell in the tents of wickedness"* (Psalm 84:10). Peter and John felt it when they said to their captors, *"We cannot stop speaking of what we have seen and heard"* (Acts 4:20). This is the kind of gut-level drive you will need to plant a new church.

ADEQUACY

The Bible cites roughly 25 qualifications (attached below) for the elder. Scripture is emphatic that these are essential qualities for the man of God who will lead a local congregation. These are baseline character qualifications for anyone serving in pastoral ministry. Those considering a calling to pastoral ministry should carefully and prayerfully study <u>1 Timothy 3</u> and <u>Titus 1</u>, and compare their lives to the standards of those passages. In addition to the scriptural qualifications given in God's Word, there are some secondary qualities commonly found in fruitful church planters. Scripture does not mandate these qualities, thus you should not consider them mandatory, either. However, it is wise for aspiring church planters who lack these qualities to work diligently to develop these areas, and seek the help of those who obviously possess them.

AFFIRMATION

Affirmation of a sending church itself is the indispensable third confirmation. Though some may believe God is calling them to plant a new church, if the elders and members of the current church do not agree with them, this is a major red flag and should result in slowing down the church planting process (if not ending it all together). The local church is the means by which God will expand his kingdom.

Denominations and para-church organizations are tremendous resources for the church planter, and should be utilized to the extent that they are helpful. However, these organizations cannot replace the local church as the central authority in the establishment and renewal of the local church. Potential planters should seek help from godly individuals who know them well, and employ them to give an honest assessment of their weaknesses. They should ask them difficult questions such as: "Do you consider me to be self-controlled?" "Do you think I am a good manager of my household?" Encourage them to listen to the answers given and to take the suggestions and evaluations to heart.

Know Your Role

Can you still help start churches even if you are not called to be a Church Planter? *Yes.* Becoming a church planter is not the only way people can help to start new churches. For many, joining a church planting team is a very tangible way to help start new churches. Church planting teams are often in need of committed Christians to serve in key ministry leadership positions. Take a few minutes to look over the examples below to see if your gifts and talents could be of use to a church planting team.

Prayer Advocate

The Prayer Advocate is responsible for promoting personal and corporate prayer in the life of a new church. This person should (1) maintain a healthy and growing spiritual life and lead others to do the same; (2) establish a monthly church-wide prayer meeting for members and attenders; (3) create an efficient means of communicating time sensitive prayer concerns to the congregation; (4) create an efficient means of communicating church prayer needs to key supporters and partners; and (5) work with other ministry leaders to ensure that prayer plays a key role in their ministries.

Worship Leader

The Worship Leader is responsible for magnifying the greatness of God and Jesus Christ through the planning, conducting, and promotion of the music and worship programs of a church. This person should (1) maintain a healthy and growing spiritual life and lead others to do the same; (2) participate regularly in leading worship music at gatherings on Sundays and at other events from time to time; (3) recruit, develop, and lead a worship team; (4) work with pastors to select worship song sets that are gospel-centered and Christ-exalting; (5) establish and lead rehearsals; and (6) help in the oversight and coordination of other areas related to worship – sound, lights, video, etc.

Discipleship Director

The Discipleship Director is responsible for promoting discipleship in a church to help people grow in both knowledge of and obedience to the Word of God. This person should (1) maintain a healthy and growing spiritual life and lead others to do the same; (2) equip mature Christians with the tools and resources necessary to disciple others; (3) identify less mature Christians in need of discipleship; and (4) establish and facilitate disciple-making relationships throughout the congregation.

Outreach Coordinator

The Outreach Coordinator is responsible for the overall planning, development, and deployment of the outreach ministries of a new church, including the local, national, and international mission fields. This person should (1) maintain a healthy and growing spiritual life and lead others to do the same; (2) develop and maintain local and international mission programs; (3) recruit, train, and support a network of volunteers to lead various outreach opportunities; (4) plan and lead mission trips, both locally and abroad; (5) work with church leadership to establish a presence for the church at community events; and (6) network with various small groups and individuals to accomplish the outreach goals of the congregation.

Children's Ministry Coordinator

The Children's Ministry Coordinator is responsible for the planning, conducting, promoting, and evaluating a comprehensive and balanced ministry to a children and their families. This person should (1) maintain a healthy and growing spiritual life and lead others to do the same; (2) plan programs and activities for the spiritual, emotional, and intellectual development of our children and their parents or guardians; (3) enlist and equip ministry leadership and volunteers; (4) evaluate and secure literature, resources, and teaching material; (5) develop and implement policies for the safety and security of the children: and (6) coordinate and staff the care of young children during worship services and special church-wide events.

Communications Coordinator

The Communications Coordinator is responsible for ensuring that the media and message of a church is consistent, biblical, and clear. This person should (1) maintain a healthy and growing spiritual life and lead others to do the same; (2) manage content and aesthetics for all forms of church communication including web, social media, and print; (3) act as the funnel through which all communications pass before being released; (4) work with various ministry heads to produce a consistent, articulate message to the community and to the congregation; (5) manage the church membership database, keeping track of visitors and those who attend outreach events hosted by the church; (6) regularly inspect the website for outdated information and broken links; (7) provide content for any of the church's social media posts or campaigns; and (8) ensure that the church is utilizing the best communication methods available to reach the largest number of members and attenders.

TECHNICAL DIRECTOR

The Technical Director is responsible for leading a team of volunteers to provide high quality support for audio, video, and lighting used during worship gatherings and other events as needed. This person should (1) maintain a healthy and growing spiritual life and lead others to do the same; (2) recruit volunteers; (3)

provide training opportunities for volunteers to gain the necessary skill set for success in their area; (4) initiate and plan ongoing training on a regular basis; (5) schedule the needed volunteers for each service or event and communicate their responsibilities in advance; (6) initiate repairs and replacements for critical equipment; and (7) establish a plan to prepare and execute quality video, display, and lighting elements for each service or event.

Service Coordinator

The Service Coordinator is responsible for planning, implementing, and evaluating the church worship services including service formats, order, themes, and special programs. This person should (1) maintain a healthy and growing spiritual life and lead others to do the same; (2) manage the logistics of all worship services; (3) work alongside the preaching pastor and the service leaders to create a cohesive presentation of service elements; (4) act as the point of contact for all elements of the worship service; and (5) develop a team and a system that will keep everyone involved informed.

STUDENT MINISTRY DIRECTOR

The Student Ministry Director is responsible for planning, conducting, promoting, and evaluating a comprehensive and balanced ministry to youth and their families. This person should (1) maintain a healthy and growing spiritual life and lead others to do the same; (2) plan programs and activities for the spiritual, emotional, and intellectual development of youth and their parents or guardians; (3) enlist and equip ministry leadership and volunteers; (4) evaluate and secure literature, resources, and teaching material; (4) develop and implement policies for the safety and security of youth; (5) plan and conduct special projects, such as camps and retreats; and (6) coordinate youth outreach and mission trips.

TREASURER

The Treasurer is responsible for properly receiving, dispersing, accounting, and safeguarding church funds within policies established by the church. This person should (1) maintain a healthy and growing spiritual life and lead others to do the same; (2) develop and implement policies and procedures related to receiving, accounting, and dispersing church funds; (3) maintain records of funds received and dispersed; (4) enlist volunteers to receive, count, and deposit money; (5) maintain records of contributions and prepare and distribute contribution statements; (6) reconcile monthly bank statements and correct ledgers as needed; and (7) make regular reports to the church or leadership as directed by church policies.

Small Group Coordinator

The Small Group Coordinator is responsible for organizing the small group ministry for the development and care of disciples, the encouragement of biblical community, and the ministry to the lost. This person should (1) maintain a healthy and growing spiritual life and lead others to do the same; (2) collaborate with church leadership to build and implement a system of small groups; (3) develop and implement procedures that promote attendance and participation in small groups; (4) be familiar with curriculum resources and make recommendations for classes and groups; (5) recruit and develop leadership for future groups; (6) provide accountability and further training for current small group leaders.

These are just a few of what could be dozens more positions that are needed in new churches. As God calls individuals to lead the forming of new churches, seriously consider how you can be involved. Certainly there are meaningful ways to be involved at a distance through prayer, financial support, and volunteerism, but nothing will cause you to grow as a Christian like striving together with a team of likeminded Christians to establish a new church in a community that needs one.

Church Planter Testimony:
James Hinton

My name is James Hinton, I am 42 years old, I have 7 wonderful kids, and a beautiful wife. I love Jesus, I love serving the church, but I have a career-type job as a federal agent that, I thought, somewhat precluded me from church planting. I thought I should leave that to the professionals.

In 2012, God began to stir in my heart about church planting, and about the need for multiple churches being planted especially in the Shenandoah Valley. For us it was wanting to be a part of something God was going to do in a special and unique way, and church planting became the catalyst for that. I was involved as a Men's Pastor in men's ministry, and began realizing that the key to effective, strong churches was strong men, which was such a gap in Christian circles; you just didn't have them. Most men didn't know what a real man was, nor how to explain what a man was effectively, Biblically, or redemptively.

From the very beginning of our church plant, God began to lead in us to build from the ground up a church whose foundation, focus, thrust—everything that this church was going to accomplish was going to be accomplished through Gospel-centered masculinity; it was going to be accomplished through men.

That was our push to get us into the church planting context. We were just average Joe's that, because of the Gospel, we have something extraordinary to share.

What I found is that, as we started reaching the average Joe's and as we started reaching into our community, God started using my professional environment, whether as a combat instructor or firearms instructor to draw in some of those men that churches otherwise wouldn't reach. I think that what helped in our church in particular is for men to hear us talking about, while having jobs that most men would really find appealing, what is really appealing is the Gospel, and to hear us saying to them, "Christ is far better than anything that this world has to offer, including any job, any prestige, any position, and any power or influence. All of that means nothing in comparison to what is given you in Christ."

From the very beginning, we wanted to plant a church and continue to have me work my job. We wanted to use my vocation professionally for God to use redemptively. Our profession is ministry. We're on mission when we're at home; we're on mission when we're at the workplace. Part of the goal for us was demystifying ministry, how ministry was done, and simplifying the process. I wanted my people to understand we don't have to be like the big church on the corner. What I needed to do was make disciples. That's what church planting is, making disciples.

We don't do ministry stuff, and then family stuff. We do ministry stuff while we are living as family. Simply what we have done at our church is to invite families and people to come along with us as we live as a family. Ultimately, our goal is to help people go further, farther, faster—to take what we have learned and done wrong, and let them learn from those experience and move beyond that. Particularly, we never wanted to create a mega-church. We wanted to plant a church that would plant more churches throughout the Shenandoah Valley, and wherever God would want us to send people to that are going to do what we do. What we do is simplify ministry, make it communicable, transferable, and to make sure it is reproducible in a way that makes sense for the context.

We started Mosaic with 9 people: my wife, myself, and our 7 kids. We didn't have any funding, we didn't have the things that church plants typically want to have, but what we did have was relational context and community. Others may not have what they think a "professional pastor" needs, but God is sovereign and has given individuals what they need to do what He has called them to do. Most likely, that may mean he has given them a church planting context. Now, that church plant may look different than some other guy that just finished his M. Div. at seminary, but that doesn't mean your church is any less valuable.

The fact that I get to call myself, not "Special Agent Hinton," but James Hinton, a child of God, because of my relationship with Him, because of the fact that I am his son, that moves me to do things that don't make sense. Chances are, you might be reading this thinking that church planting doesn't make sense to you right now. It's not supposed to make sense. The mission mandated to share the Gospel with all the world doesn't make sense. It's not supposed to be quantified. It's just supposed to be obeyed. Step out, and you'll figure out the details as you go.

God is sovereign, He is in control and He empowers our steps as we move forward with our King. It is not going out on your own trying to blaze a trail. It is simply a matter of obeying Jesus as He leads you on His Great Mission. The reality is, He is on mission to win the world to himself. He just invites us to come along and play. It's a great thing to be on His team because, in the end, we win.

Conclusion

I have sought to persuade you in this little book that your life is well spent involved in church planting. Every Christian should consider giving themselves to the spread of the gospel: leading a church planting initiative, or supporting one. If you are wondering what to do next from here, let me encourage you to set up a time to talk with your local church leaders about it. Churches plant churches, and current church leaders are the best assessors of future church leaders. Start your journey with a conversation with those that lead your current church.

You may be tempted with a number of feelings that discourage you from participating in planting after reading this book:

- *I do not have any gifts a church plant could use.*
- *I am not a leader.*
- *I do not know if my family could handle it.*
- *[Insert some other insecurity]*

I want to remove every hurdle Satan might use to keep you from the joy that there is in spreading the gospel and building God's church. Would you like a really, really easy place to start? **Consider going through the online course that accompanies this book: newcityplanting.org/primer.** If you are a church congregant, consider going to your closest friends and share with them about this new burden for church planting, and ask them if they will take the course with you.

If you are a pastor of a church that is not currently involved in church planting, consider taking your key leaders through this course. If you have further questions about how to get involved, please email me at info@newcityplanting.net. It is never too late to put your hand to the plow, and start planting churches.

If you have a grasp on everything I covered in this book, pick up *Church Planting Thresholds: A Gospel Centered Guide.* New City Network has made this book available at a low cost for bulk orders. All proceeds go to furthering the work of church planting. *Thresholds* is a practical, step-by-step guide through the planting process—from calling to planting churches that plants churches. You can find *Thresholds* at newcityplanting.org/thresholds, or on Amazon.com.

Wherever you are in your journey with Christ, I pray that you would consider joining God's work in the world through church planting. It is never too late or too early to play some role in fulfilling the final marching orders of King Jesus.

Endnotes

1. Mark Dever and Jonathan Leeman, *Understanding the Great Commission* (Nashville, TN: B&H Publishing Group, 2016), "Chapter 10," Electronic Format.

2. Susan Malphurs, "15 Reasons Why Committed Christians Do Not Attend Church," *The Malphurs Group Blog, The Malphurs Group: Envision Tomorrow Today*, September 21, 2015, accessed August 1, 2016, http://www.malphursgroup.com/15-reasons-why-committed-christians-do-not-attend-church/.

3. Ted Kluck and Kevin DeYoung, "Church: Love It, Don't Leave It," *onfaith* (blog), *faithstreet*, n.d., accessed August 1, 2016, http://www.faithstreet.com/onfaith/2009/07/01/church-love-it-dont-leave-it/123.

4. Dave Bruskas. "Churches Planting Churches Biblically," *ChurchLeaders* (blog), n.d., accessed July 28, 2016, http://www.churchleaders.com/outreach-missions/outreach-missions-

blogs/146052-churches-planting-churches-biblically.html.

5. Spurgeon, Charles. "The Waterer Watered," Metropolitan Tabernacle, Newington, England. A Sunday Sermon; April 23, 1865. Accessed November 23, 2016. http://www.biblebb.com/files/spurgeon/0626.htm

6. David T. Olson, *The American Church in Crisis: Groundbreaking Research Based on a National Database of over 200,000 Churches.* Grand Rapids, Mich.: Zondervan, 2008. 16.

7. Steve McSwain, "Why Nobody Wants to Go to Church Anymore," *The Blog, The Huffington Post,* October 14, 2013, accessed July 28, 2016, http://www.huffingtonpost.com/steve-mcswain/why-nobody-wants-to-go-to_b_4086016.html.

8. Ibid.

9. Olson. *The American Church in Crisis.* 16.

10. Ed Stetzer and Phillip Connor. "Church Plant Survivability and Health Study 2007." North American Mission Board. 2007. Accessed January 8, 2016.

11. Thom Rainer. "Thirteen Issues for Churches in 2013: Issues 1-6." *Thom Rainer: Growing Healthy Churches. Together.* (blog), n.d., Accessed January 8, 2016. http://thomrainer.com/2012/12/thirteen-issues-for-churches-in-2013-issues-1-6/.

12. Aubrey Malphurs, "The State of the American Church: Plateaued or Declining," *The Malphurs Group Blog, The Malphurs Group: Envision Tomorrow Today,* September 5, 2014, accessed July 28, 2016, http://www.malphursgroup.com/state-of-the-american-church-plateaued-declining/.

13. Ed Stetzer, "The Explosive Growth of U.S. Megachurches, Even While Many Say Their Day is Done" February 19, 2013. (Christianitytoday.com)

14. Thom Rainer, "One Key Reason Most Churches Do Not Exceed 350 in Average Attendance," *Thom Rainer: Growing Healthy Churches. Together.* (blog), March 25, 2015, accessed July 28, 2016, http://thomrainer.com/2015/03/one-key-reason-churches-exceed-350-average-attendance/.

15. Kelly Shattuck, "7 Startling Facts: An up Close Look at Church Attendance in America," *Church Leaders* (blog), accessed July 28, 2016, http://www.churchleaders.com/pastors/pastor-articles/139575-7-startling-facts-an-up-close-look-at-church-attendance-in-america.html.

16. Ibid.

17. Mark A. Noll, *A History of Christianity in the United States and Canada.* Grand Rapids, MI: W.B. Eerdmans Publishing Co., 1992.

18. Steve Addison, "Rapid Mobilization, How the West Was Won," *Mission Frontiers* (blog), July 1, 2015, accessed July 28, 2016, http://

www.missionfrontiers.org/issue/article/rapid-mobilization.

19. John Piper, *Brothers, We are Not Professionals.* B&H Publishing Group, Nashville, TN. 2013, 1

20. Emma Green, "Baptists, Just Without the Baptisms" May 14, 2014 (theatlantic.com)

21. Tim Keller. "Why Church Planting?" A blog adapted from an article titled, "Why Plant Churches." January 9, 2012. Accessed December 14, 2016. http://www.acts29.com/why-church-planting/

22. David Phillips, "Church Planting Tutorial: 7. Church Planting Models," *PASSION4PLANTING* (blog), accessed July 28, 2016, http://church-planting.net/church-planting-tutorial-church-planting-models/.

23. Frank Viola, *Finding Organic Church: A Comprehensive Guide to Starting and Sustaining Authentic Christian Communities.* 2009 David C. Cook Publishing

24. Joseph Henry Thayer and Carl Ludwig Wilibald Grimm. "ὀρέγω: Strongs G3713." *Thayer's Greek-English Lexicon of the New Testament: Coded with Strong's Concordance Numbers.* Sixth Printing. ed. Peabody, Mass.: Hendrickson, 2003.

25. Ibid. "πιθυμέω: Strongs G1937."

Made in the USA
Columbia, SC
17 December 2018